D1233168

COOL CATS

Ocicats

by Betsy Rathburn

BLASTOFF! READERS

2

BELLWETHER MEDIA • MINNEAPOLIS, MN

Note to Librarians, Teachers, and Parents:

Blastoff! Readers are carefully developed by literacy experts and combine standards-based content with developmentally appropriate text.

Level 1 provides the most support through repetition of high-frequency words, light text, predictable sentence patterns, and strong visual support.

Level 2 offers early readers a bit more challenge through varied simple sentences, increased text load, and less repetition of high-frequency words.

Level 3 advances early-fluent readers toward fluency through increased text and concept load, less reliance on visuals, longer sentences, and more literary language.

Level 4 builds reading stamina by providing more text per page, increased use of punctuation, greater variation in sentence patterns, and increasingly challenging vocabulary.

Level 5 encourages children to move from "learning to read" to "reading to learn" by providing even more text, varied writing styles, and less familiar topics.

Whichever book is right for your reader, Blastoff! Readers are the perfect books to build confidence and encourage a love of reading that will last a lifetime!

This edition first published in 2017 by Bellwether Media, Inc.

No part of this publication may be reproduced in whole or in part without written permission of the publisher. For information regarding permission, write to Bellwether Media, Inc., Attention: Permissions Department, 5357 Penn Avenue South, Minneapolis, MN 55419.

Library of Congress Cataloging-in-Publication Data

Names: Rathburn, Betsy, author.
Title: Ocicats / by Betsy Rathburn.
Other titles: Blastoff! Readers. 2, Cool Cats.
Description: Minneapolis, MN : Bellwether Media, Inc., [2017] | Series: Blastoff! Readers. Cool Cats | Audience: Ages 5-8. | Audience: K to grade 3. | Includes bibliographical references and index.
Identifiers: LCCN 2016032033 (print) | LCCN 2016040360 (ebook) | ISBN 9781626175631 (hardcover : alk. paper) | ISBN 9781681032849 (ebook)
Subjects: LCSH: Ocicat–Juvenile literature. | Cat breeds–Juvenile literature.
Classification: LCC SF449.O35 R38 2017 (print) | LCC SF449.O35 (ebook) | DDC 636.8/2–dc23
LC record available at https://lccn.loc.gov/2016032033

Text copyright © 2017 by Bellwether Media, Inc. BLASTOFF! READERS and associated logos are trademarks and/or registered trademarks of Bellwether Media, Inc. SCHOLASTIC, CHILDREN'S PRESS, and associated logos are trademarks and/or registered trademarks of Scholastic Inc.

Editor: Christina Leaf   Designer: Lois Stanfield

Printed in the United States of America, North Mankato, MN.

Table of Contents

What Are Ocicats?

Ocicats are large, **striking** cats. Their spotted **coats** make them look wild.

But they are friendly
and playful.

5

Ocicats have short, soft hair that covers their **athletic** bodies.

They are named after wild cats called ocelots.

The **breed** started in Michigan in 1964. Virginia Daly **bred** an Abyssinian with a Siamese cat.

Michigan

N
W ✦ E
S

Abyssinian ↓   Siamese ↓

The kittens were later bred to
another Abyssinian. The result was
a spotted kitten named Tonga.

People loved Tonga's unusual pattern. More cats were bred to look like him.

Today, people are still wild about ocicats!

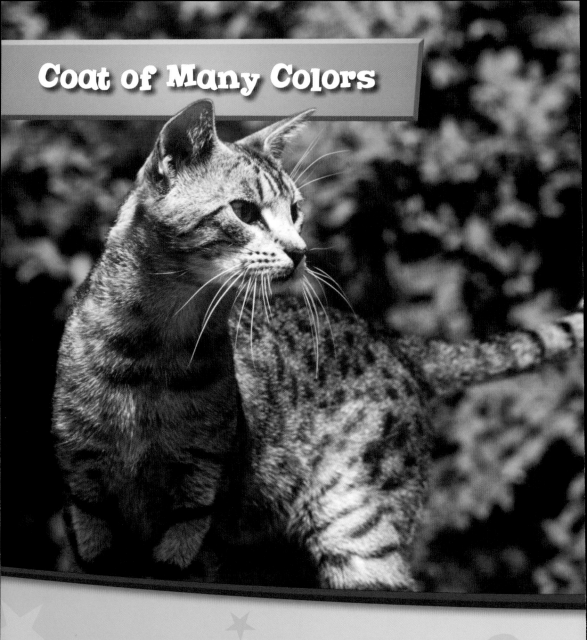

Coat of Many Colors

Ocicats come in 12 colors. Chocolate is common. **Tawny** and blue are also popular colors.

Ocicat Coats

chocolate

tawny

blue

cinnamon

Ocicat tails have dark tips. The tip tells the cat's true coat color.

Most ocicats are spotted. **Tabby** and **ticked** coats have become less common as the breed grows.

Solid ocicats have ghost spots.
These are hard to see.

Ocicats have big, **slanted** eyes.
These come in any color but blue.
Strong legs help the cats jump
high and climb tall furniture.

Ocicat Profile

— large, slanted eyes

spotted coat

athletic body —

long tail with dark tip

Weight: 6 to 15 pounds (3 to 7 kilograms)

Life Span: 15 to 18 years

Ocicats are **intelligent** cats that love to play. Puzzle toys keep them **entertained**.

Some even learn to open lids to get treats!

Ocicats like to be around humans. They follow their owners around.

Some ocicats will greet
strangers at the door!

Glossary

athletic—being strong, fit, and active

bred—purposely mated two cats to make kittens with certain qualities

breed—a type of cat

coats—the hair or fur covering some animals

entertained—kept busy and interested

intelligent—able to learn and be trained

slanted—at an angle

solid—one color

striking—beautiful or unusual in a way that calls for attention

tabby—a pattern that has stripes, patches, or swirls of colors

tawny—light brown

ticked—having many lines of colors

To Learn More

AT THE LIBRARY
Felix, Rebecca. *Abyssinians*. Minneapolis, Minn.: Bellwether Media, 2016.

Mattern, Joanne. *Ocicats*. Mankato, Minn.: Capstone Press, 2011.

Murray, Julie. *Ocicat Cats*. Edina, Minn.: Abdo Pub., 2003.

ON THE WEB
Learning more about ocicats is as easy as 1, 2, 3.

1. Go to www.factsurfer.com.

2. Enter "ocicats" into the search box.

3. Click the "Surf" button and you will see a list of related web sites.

With factsurfer.com, finding more information is just a click away.

Index

The images in this book are reproduced through the courtesy of: Tierfotoagentur/ R. Richter/ Alamy, front cover; Juniors/ Juniors/ SuperStock, pp. 4-5, 13 (upper left and lower right); Tierfotoagentur/ Alamy, pp. 5, 10 (cats); 13 (lower left) 15, 20-21; Shattil & Rozinski/ Nature Picture Library, p. 6; Juniors Bildarchiv GmbH/ Alamy, pp. 6-7, 11; Nikolai Tsvetkov, p. 8 (right); Karin Langner-Bahmann/ Wikicommons, p. 8 (left); Tierfotoagentur/ Age Fotostock, pp. 8-9 (cat), 18; SJ Travel Photo, pp. 8-9 (background); Room27, p. 10 (background); Animals Animals/ SuperStock, pp. 12-13; Tom Bjornstad/ Wikicommons, p. 13 (upper right); Klein-Hubert/ KimballStock, p. 14; Marka/ Marka/ SuperStock, pp. 16-17; Helmi Flick/ Animal-Photography, p. 17; BlueValentines/ Imagebroker/ FLPA, p. 19 (subject); Charts and BG, p. 19 (background); Juniors Bildarchiv/ Age Fotostock, p. 20.